Volume 8

BRITISH RAILWAYS IN COLOUR

Alan Earnshaw

FROM STEAM
TO THE SCRAPYARD

D1368864

Nostalgia Road Publications

The **British Railways In Colour** Series ™

is produced under license by

Nostalgia Road Publications Ltd.

Units 5-8, Chancel Place

Shap Road Industrial Estate, Kendal LA9 6NZ

Tel. 01539 738832 - Fax: 01539 730075

designed and published by

Trans-Pennine Publishing Ltd.

PO Box 10,
Appleby-in-Westmorland,
Cumbria, CA16 6FA
Tel. 017683 51053 Fax. 017683 53558
e-mail: admin@transpenninepublishing.co.uk

and printed by

Kent Valley Colour Printers Ltd.

Kendal, Cumbria
01539 741344

© Trans-Pennine Publishing Ltd. 2004
Photographs: As credited

Front Cover: Just one of the many Stanier 8F 2-8-0s that were brought to account by Alfred Draper of Hull, is seen in August of 1967. *John Gill* (M500)

Rear Cover Top: The familiar scene witnessed by all of those who made the pilgrimage to Barry in the 1960s! This was the view in 1967 after an influx of redundant Bulleid Pacifics. *Win Wall, Strathwood Library Collection* (S301)

Rear Cover Bottom: The now valuable cabside numberplates are still intact on 1451, but the cab roof has already gone. Evidence of torch activity along the tanks of this Collett 0-4-2T at Swindon's infamous 'C Shop' shows that it is unlikely to last much longer than August 1964. *The late Norman Browne; Strathwood Library Collection* (W402)

Title Page: An unidentified 9F has arrived for the last post at Birds of Long Marston in 1968. *John Fernyhaugh* (B300)

This Page: Part of the continuation of the GWR's build program of Hawksworth-designed Pannier Tank engines continued into the BR era. One of these, 8403, has only had a short working life before arriving at Ward's yard in Briton Ferry where she is seen on 18th August 1965. *Douglas Paul* (W409)

ISBN 1 903016 49 5
British Cataloguing in Publication Data
A catalogue record for this book is available from the British Library

WELCOME to the eighth volume of the **British Railways in Colour** series, which deals with the disposal of the British Railways steam locomotive fleet in the decade from 1959 to 1968.

The sad story surrounding the demise of the British Railway steam locomotive fleet continues to attract considerable attention, despite it now being almost 12 years since I wrote the book *Steam For Scrap – The Complete Story*.

Above: *In the late 1950s and early '60s, the works at Stratford quickly chopped up engines after they had been withdrawn. Some may have been cut up before 'spotters' even saw their withdrawal notices in the enthusiast's press of the day. Here we have Class J20 64697 and Class N7/3 69728 as they wait for processing at Stratford in October 1961.*
The late Norman Browne;
Strathwood Library Collection (E381)

Yet, despite the grand title envisaged by my publisher of that time, this could never have hoped to tell the full account of how British Railways disposed of thousands of steam engines between 1st January 1948 and 31st August 1968. Steam came to an official end on British Railways over the weekend of 3rd – 4th August 1968, with the remaining steam sheds (all in the North West of England) closing on Monday 5th August. Two weeks later BR ran a 'farewell to steam' railtour over the Settle & Carlisle route, which was called the Fifteen Guinea special.

What steam fan of the time wouldn't have wanted to go on this special, but by virtue of the fact that it was Fifteen Guineas (to me three week's wages), there wasn't a cat in you know where's chance of my actually riding upon it! Even for a skilled man, Fifteen Guineas (or £15 15s) was a full week's wage in those days!

Furthermore there were only a limited number of seats on the special, so if you had to think about saving for it, there was no point, because by the time you had done so, all the seats would have sold out anyway! I did however get to see it from the lofty heights of Whernside, where several of us were taking part in a mountain rescue team exercise.

We watched in awe as a telltale plume of smoke came into view from behind Simon Fell below Ingleborough, before Britannia Class Pacific 70013 *Oliver Cromwell* came into view. It was one of those lasting and majestic moments as we watched it curve over Ribblehead Viaduct and through Blea Moor Sidings way below us. Yet, few of the spectators or travellers back then could have ever believed that one day, steam would return to periodically work the S&C or any other operational British Railway line come to that.

It is true that people were making valiant efforts to privately purchase locomotives for preservation, and the National Collection was claiming others for display as 'museum pieces'! Yet few of us ever imagined that schemes like the Bluebell Railway and the Keighley & Worth Valley (which had re-opened a few weeks earlier) would ever amount to very much. All too common was the daily sight of locomotives dumped at engine sheds or in old sidings, as they were progressively sent to private scrap yards for disposal.

The reasons why so many locomotives were withdrawn and sent to scrap is fully detailed in our companion book, *British Railways in Colour Vol.7 – Steam For Sale*. This book therefore pre-supposes that the reader will have read that account prior to this one.

This publication cannot hope to go into the full details of the scrapping programme, and even mammoth works like Peter Hands' *What Happened To Steam?* series was fraught with many problems. The trouble is, that not all engines died where they were supposed to, and the only sure record of any locomotive's demise is a photographic record of where and when its end occurred. Yet, as my Picture Editor, Kevin Derrick warns me, 'it can still be dangerous to assume that the photographer's records are 100% correct.'

This book is not a continuation of the *Steam For Scrap* series, but a representative look at how BR engines were scrapped, and it does so by looking at the facts behind the process, considering how Beeching's plans *The Re-shaping of British Railways* and the *British Railways Workshops Plan* impacted on the subject.

There is no attempt to cover every locomotive, nor indeed every class or scrapyard, but what I hope to show is the next stage in my research and move on from the original books that were, except for the covers, illustrated only by monochrome pictures. The pictures here (from the Strathwood and Trans-Pennine collections) all speak volumes and I only wish that a fraction of them had been available to us back in the 1980s.

The subject is not the happiest one for a steam locomotive enthusiast to read, let alone research and write, but it is a part of our social history. Indeed, we are already planning a companion history, which details the resurrection and new service lives of those steam engines that we all thought had gone for good back in 1968.

Obviously, we need the co-operation of our readers to develop that series, and would be delighted to hear from all those who have been concerned with the restoration of locomotives over the past 35 years or so. Your photographs and memories will be a vital ingredient in the success of the books that will follow.

Alan Earnshaw   Appleby-in-Westmorland June 2004

Above: *A collector's dream, as both the smokebox plate of T9 Class 4-4-0 30284 and (remarkably) the 71A Eastleigh shed plate are seen at Eastleigh Works on 9th January 1959.* Strathwood Library Collection (S302)

Anyone who has ever studied the subject of the disposal of British steam can only come to one decision: namely it was a sheer waste of money. No matter how you arrive at the conclusion (whether you believe the BR Standard steam locomotives were built too late, or that the overall end of steam came too early), it is impossible to dismiss just how much money was actually squandered in the period concerned.

There is an argument that takes us back to 1957, and the Conservative government's edict that the railways should reach overall profitability within five years, or by 1962 in other words. When it was clear that the railways had no chance of achieving this, Richard Beeching was appointed to write a report that would 'rubber stamp' the mass closures that would logically follow.

A variety of authors have covered the Beeching era in great depth, and they have come up with many different conclusions. Yet it is significant that Beeching was an accountant, and his remit was simply to look at the financial state of the railways, and take steps for them to reach the goal of overall profitability! This could not happen overnight, and it would not be until 1st June 1961, that Beeching would succeed Lord Robertson of Oakridge as Chairman of the British Transport Commission and do so on what was then a staggering salary of £14,000 per annum.

Top Left: *Stored at Glasgow's Corkerhill shed (67A) on 19th January 1960, but not officially withdrawn until May that year, we find McIntosh 439 Class 2P 0-4-4T 55219. Destined for one of the Scottish works, this engine still carries a tempting builder's plate for any discerning collector who might be both willing and far-sighted enough to make a modest investment!* Frank Hornby (M501)

Bottom Left: *The scandal of cutting up the BR Standards was not an isolated example of the lack of planning by BR, as a substantial number of steam engines were built in the post-war era to designs introduced by the Big Four companies. One of the engines from this period is a 94xx Class 0-6-0 Pannier Tank (9420), seen in December 1964. This Swindon creation has returned to its birthplace where it waits with 56xx Class 0-6-2Ts and a Castle on the scrap line surrounded by the debris of fallen comrades.* The late Norman Browne; Strathwood Library Collection (W408)

Top Right: *The dump at Chaddesden was built up to provide storage for the works at Derby, which was then buckling under the pressure of storing so many 'dead' engines. One of those was this ex-Midland Railway 2P Class 4-4-0 and its Jinty stable mate (47299) sometime during 1960. Peter Hands' classic series of books* What Happened To Steam *suggests 40601 ended her days at the former Great Central (LNER) works at Gorton in Manchester during January 1961. Either way, there will be no refuge for this engine that had once been a Somerset & Dorset line regular.* John Gill (M502)

At the end of 1961 BR's passenger income was £157.4 million per annum, and its freight traffic almost double this at £306.7 million. Yet, throughout its many different sectors, the British Transport Commission had an income of £710.8 million and expenses of £787 million, giving a total deficit of £65,931,337. This cost around £1.26 million every week, which whilst being a substantial sum, was nowhere near the £6.2 million that was then spent weekly on defence.

The Gross National Product for 1962 was around £23 billion, and the cost of a nationalised transport system at just under £66 million was therefore minuscule. However, you can make figures look like whatever you want, and as we argued in Volume 7 of this series, the demise of British Railways was a political act.

There was a financial case to argue for a diminution in the size of the railway network, but hindsight shows no justification of the mass slaughter that followed Beeching's *The Re-Shaping of British Railways* and the wholesale cuts that followed it in 1963. Whilst these cuts related to running miles and stations, the impact on locomotive stocks was also closely related. At the end of 1961, the first year in which BR built no new steam engines, the book value of the steam fleet was said to be £34,276,000.

Inside seven years, this asset had been scrapped for a fraction of its value, and the table below shows the numbers of steam locomotives in stock at the various years' end.

1961	1962	1963	1964	1965	1966	1967	1968
11,691	8,767	7,050	4,973	2,987	1,689	362	3

Top Left: *Like the GWR 94XX class that was perpetuated into the second half of the 1940s, we now see an LNER counterpart. First introduced in 1945 and built into the post-nationalisation age, many of Thompson's L1 2-6-4 tank engines were to be displaced within a decade by the diesel railcars built in the second half of the 1950s; again revealing either the lack of planning or not making the most of the assets available. Here, the first physical cuts have been made into 67738 ex-New England (34E) at Darlington North Road in 1962. Furthermore, it seems that no thought was given to the disposal of asbestos on steam engines at this time.* John Gill (E392)

Bottom Left: *Elegant to the end, this LMS-built 4P 4-4-0, is a victim of the 'modernisation' scheme that envisaged the demise of all four-coupled main line engines. Found in the scrap line at Derby, 41173 has already been stripped of coal and plates! However, around this time a decision was taken to ship all the 4Ps to private yards, even those that were partially cut up, so this 4P ended her days at nearby Looms of Spondon in August 1961. However the signs of her 32-month wait after withdrawal are showing through the paintwork as our photographer caught during his visit.* John Gill (M509)

Top Right: *Stripped of former honours and sandwiched between a pair of condemned Black Fives, Britannia 4-6-2, 70012* John of Gaunt *awaits entry to Ward's premises at Killamarsh near Rotherham. The date is March 1968.* Trans Pennine Archive (B301)

By the end of 1967, the value of the locomotive fleet was £273,571,000; this includes diesel, electric and multiple unit stock, but the Annual Accounts do not differentiate between them. Interestingly, these accounts do not show the sums received for the scrapped locomotives either, but the scrap prices of £2,500 for a main line express locomotive and £1,500 for a tank engine seems to be average.

Given that almost 12,000 locomotives vanished between 1961 and 1968, we might be generous and estimate total receipts of around £30,000,000. Yet, when 70000 *Britannia* had been built in 1951, it alone had cost £20,114, whilst the whole class had cost taxpayers £1,168,378 (an aggregate of £21,243 per engine). As near as can be determined, the price received for the 53 scrapped engines was £119,250.

In fact the 53 scrapped Britannias had cost £1,049,128 and given an aggregate service life of just 14.5 years each. The longest lived was of course 70013 *Oliver Cromwell*, with 17 years 3 months on BR, whereas 70050 *Firth of Clyde* managed a mere 12 years. The first of the class to go was 70007 *Coeur-de-Lion*, which fell at Crewe in 1965.

As a matter of interest, the disposal of the Britannia Class makes interesting reading, and whilst it is impossible to consider every class in this way, the notes that follow are most useful in identifying the sheer volume of waste that the railways were to experience in the mad scramble to divest itself of steam locomotives. But please bear in mind, these locomotives could all have been expected to have service lives of between 30 and 50 years.

Britannia Class Service & Disposal Record

(With Acknowledgement to The Railway Correspondence & Travel Society book *British Railways Standard Steam Locomotives* Volume 1.)

No.	Name	Entered Service	Withdrawn From Service	Last Shed	Date Disposed	Place Scrapped
70000	*Britannia*	Jan 1951	May 1966	Newton Heath	-	Preserved
70001	*Lord Hurcomb*	Feb 1951	Sep 1966	Kingmoor	Dec 1966,	Motherwell Machinery
70002	*Geoffrey Chaucer*	Mar 1951	Jan 1967	Kingmoor	May 1967	G H Campbell, Airdrie
70003	*John Bunyan*	Mar 1951	Mar 1967	Kingmoor	Nov 1967	G H Campbell, Airdrie
70004	*William Shakespeare*	Mar 1951	Dec 1967	Kingmoor	Mar 1968	T W Ward, Inverkeithing
70005	*John Milton*	Apr 1951	Jul 1967	Kingmoor	Jan 1968	G H Campbell, Airdrie
70006	*Robert Burns*	Apr 1951	May 1967	Kingmoor	Oct 1967	J McWilliams, Shettleston
70007	*Couer-de-Lion*	Apr 1951	Jun 1965	Kingmoor	Jul 1965	Crewe Works
70008	*Black Prince*	Apr 1951	Jan 1967	Kingmoor	May 1967	G H Campbell, Airdrie
70009	*Alfred The Great*	May 1951	Jan 1967	Kingmoor	May 1967	J McWilliams, Shettleston
70010	*Owen Glendower*	May 1951	Sep 1967	Kingmoor	Jan 1968	J McWilliams, Shettleston
70011	*Hotspur*	May 1951	Dec 1967	Kingmoor	Mar 1968	J McWilliams, Shettleston
70012	*John Of Gaunt*	May 1951	Dec 1967	Kingmoor	Mar 1968	T W Ward, Killamarsh
70013	*Oliver Cromwell*	May 1951	Aug 1968	Carnforth	-	Preserved
70014	*Iron Duke*	May 1951	Dec 1967	Kingmoor	Mar 1968	T W Ward, Inverkeithing
70015	*Apollo*	Jun 1951	Aug 1967	Kingmoor	Jan 1968	J McWilliams, Shettleston
70016	*Ariel*	Jun 1951	Aug 1967	Kingmoor	Dec 1967	J McWilliams, Shettleston
70017	*Arrow*	Jun 1951	Oct 1966	Kingmoor	Jan 1967	Cashmore, Newport
70018	*Flying Dutchman*	Jun 1951	Dec 1966	Kingmoor	May 1967	Motherwell Machinery
70019	*Lightning*	Jun 1951	Mar 1966	Upperby	Jun 1966	Arnott & Young, Troon
70020	*Morning Star*	Jul 1951	Jan 1967	Kingmoor	May 1967	J McWilliams, Shettleston
70021	*Mercury*	Aug 1951	Dec 1967	Kingmoor	Apr 1968	T W Ward, Inverkeithing
70022	*Tornado*	Aug 1951	Dec 1967	Kingmoor	Apr 1968	T W Ward, Inverkeithing
70023	*Venus*	Aug 1951	Dec 1967	Kingmoor	Apr 1968	T W Ward, Killamarsh
70024	*Vulcan*	Oct 1951	Dec 1967	Kingmoor	Apr 1968	T W Ward, Killamarsh
70025	*Western Star*	Sep 1952	Dec 1967	Kingmoor	Jan 1968	G H Campbell, Airdrie
70026	*Polar Star*	Oct 1952	Jan 1967	Edgeley	Apr 1967	Cashmore, Newport
70027	*Rising Star*	Oct 1952	Jul 1967	Kingmoor	Nov 1967	Motherwell Machinery
70028	*Royal Star*	Oct 1952	Sep 1967	Kingmoor	Jan 1968	J McWilliams, Shettleston
70029	*Shooting Star*	Nov 1952	Oct 1967	Kingmoor	Feb 1968	J McWilliams, Shettleston
70030	*William Wordsworth*	Nov 1952	May 1966	Upperby	Oct 1966	T W Ward, Beighton
70031	*Byron*	Nov 1952	Nov 1967	Kingmoor	Nov 1967	J McWilliams, Shettleston
70032	*Tennyson*	Dec 1952	Sep 1967	Kingmoor	Feb 1968	J McWilliams, Shettleston
70033	*Charles Dickens*	Dec 1952	Jul 1967	Kingmoor	Apr 1968	G H Campbell, Airdrie
70034	*Thomas Hardy*	Dec 1952	May 1967	Kingmoor	Sep 1967	J McWilliams, Shettleston
70035	*Rudyard Kipling*	Dec 1952	Dec 1967	Kingmoor	Mar 1968	T W Ward, Inverkeithing
70036	*Boadicea*	Dec 1952	Oct 1966	Kingmoor	Dec 1966	Motherwell Machinery
70037	*Hereward The Wake*	Dec 1952	Nov 1966	Kingmoor	Feb 1968	J McWilliams, Shettleston

Below: *A scandalous waste of money at just 13 years old, Britannia 70049* Solway Firth *has been stopped at Tyseley (2B) on 7th January 1967. The 'gallows' is not for hanging, but to instruct steam locomotive crews about clearances to the 25,000 volts electrification.* J.R.Beddows (B302)

No.	Name	Entered Service	Withdrawn From Service	Last Shed	Date Disposed	Place Scrapped
70038	*Robin Hood*	Jan 1953	Aug 1967	Kingmoor	Dec 1967	J McWilliams, Shettleston
70039	*Sir Christopher Wren*	Feb 1953	Sep 1967	Kingmoor	Jan 1968	J McWilliams, Shettleston
70040	*Clive of India*	Mar 1953	Apr 1967	Kingmoor	Nov 1967	J McWilliams, Shettleston
70041	*Sir John Moore*	Mar 1953	Apr 1967	Kingmoor	Sep 1967	J McWilliams, Shettleston
70042	*Lord Roberts*	Apr1953	May 1967	Kingmoor	Oct 1967	J McWilliams, Shettleston
70043	*Lord Kitchener*	Jun 1953	Aug 1965	Crewe South	Oct 1965	T W Ward, Beighton
70044	*Earl Haig*	Jun 1953	Oct 1966	Edgeley	Feb 1967	T W Ward, Beighton
70045	*Lord Rowallan*	Jun 1954	Dec 1967	Kingmoor	Feb 1968	T W Ward, Beighton
70046	*Anzac*	Jun 1954	Jul 1967	Kingmoor	Nov 1967	G H Campbell, Airdrie
70047	-	Jun 1954	Jul 1967	Kingmoor	Dec 1967	G H Campbell, Airdrie
70048	*The Territorial Army*	Jul 1954	May 1967	Kingmoor	Sep 1967	J McWilliams, Shettleston
70049	*Solway Firth*	Jul 1954	Dec 1967	Kingmoor	Mar 1968	J McWilliams, Shettleston
70050	*Firth of Clyde*	Aug 1954	Aug 1966	Kingmoor	Oct 1966	G H Campbell, Airdrie
70051	*Firth Of Forth*	Aug 1954	Dec 1967	Kingmoor	Mar 1968	J McWilliams, Shettleston
70052	*Firth of Tay*	Aug 1954	Apr 1967	Kingmoor	Oct 1967	G H Campbell, Airdrie
70053	*Moray Firth*	Sep 1954	Apr 1967	Kingmoor	Sep 1967	J McWilliams, Shettleston
70054	*Dornoch Firth*	Sep 1954	Nov 1966	Kingmoor	May 1967	Motherwell Machinery

Top Left: *Cashmores at Great Bridge will make short work of this ex-GWR 42xx and a trio of Prairie tanks in 1965. Ironically many of the 42xx class had been stored for a period not long after building as there was little work for them to do at the time. Even so, the GWR wanted to keep its engine builders in work and not lay them off during the Depression.*
Trans-Pennine Archive (W403)

Bottom Left: *Another GWR Prairie tank that lasted a long period in the Woodhams yard at Barry was 4156. Yet after being robbed of many parts, it was scrapped along with 92085 as part of a clean-up at the yard in July 1980. Fortunately, sister engines 4110, 4115, 4121, 4141, 4144, 4150 and 4160 would all escape Barry for preservation. Try counting the wagon wheels in the background!*
Steve Ireland Collection (W410)

Top Right: *One of the more awful and lingering types of death sentence, was the practice of being 'hung, drawn and quartered'. In this barbaric ritual, the 'victim' was hung almost to the point of death and then had his innards drawn out whilst he was still alive, before being chopped into quarters. A similar gruesome fate appears to await Stanier Black Five 44666 at the hands of Drapers 'piece rate' executioners. Along with an ex-LNER Q6 Class 0-8-0, it displays its entrails in the Hull yard. She defiantly and confusingly shows Edge Hill (8A) painted on the smokebox door as well as the neater Saltley branding on the buffer beam. By November 1967, Drapers yard was getting through engines at a healthy pace.*
John Gill (M508)

Another interesting factor to emerge from a study of BR's statistics, is the fact that the annual mileage of locomotives was not recorded after 1963. Therefore, we can gain no true evaluation of what sort of mileage the Britannias achieved. It is safe to say that none of them ever managed a million miles, and it is reputed that even 70013 only got to 900,000 miles in her 17 years on BR.

When we contrast that with other BR steam engines, we can make some interesting comparisons. Take for example the 1,318,765 miles accumulated by ex-Southern Railway Merchant Navy Class Pacific 35007 *Aberdeen Commonwealth* (itself prematurely scrapped). Realistically then, mileages of 2.5 million miles could have been expected from each of the Britannia Pacifics, but this is not the only class where wastage is observed.

The same level of 'under-use' is true right across the 999-strong BR Standard locomotive fleet, where none of the engines ever fulfilled their expected lifespan, especially in the 9F 2-10-0 heavy freight locomotive class.

Add to these 999 'Standards' the 1,538 locomotives built to 'Big Four' designs after 1st January 1948, and by the time *Evening Star* was built in 1960, BR had a fleet of 2,537 relatively new steam locomotives. Eight years later the steam stock was down to just the three narrow gauge locomotives on the Vale of Rheidol Railway. This therefore begins to show the magnitude of a politically-driven exercise, in which steam was for sale at any price. The idea of a public service obligation by the railways was also considered outdated, as more and more emphasis was put into road-building programmes.

Removing emotion and sentiment from the subject, any serious student will readily acknowledge that a question must hang over the decision to build the BR Standards. Given that so many locomotives were built to pre-BR designs, it also begs the question as to whether or not this should have remained the extent of BR's steam locomotive building policy. Those types included: -

GWR	4-6-0	Castle Class	30
GWR	4-6-0	Hall Class	49
GWR	4-6-0	Manor Class	10
GWR	0-6-0	2251 Class	2
GWR	2-6-2T	5101 Class	20
GWR	0-6-0T	15xx Class	10
GWR	0-6-0T	16xx Class	70
GWR	0-6-0T	57xx Class	41
GWR	0-6-0T	74xx Class	20
GWR	0-6-0T	94xx	220
LMS	4-6-2	Duchess Class	1
LMS	4-6-0	5MT Class	100
LMS	2-6-0	4MT Class	159
LMS	2-6-0	2MT Class	108
LMS	2-6-4T	4MT Class	147
LMS	2-6-2T	2MT Class	120
LMS	0-4-0	Dock Tank Class	5
LNER	4-6-2	A1 Class	49
LNER	4-6-2	A2 Class	14
LNER	4-6-0	B1 Class	136
LNER	2-6-0	K1 Class	70
LNER	2-6-4T	L1 Class	99
LNER	0-6-0T	J72 Class	28
SR	4-6-2	Merchant Navy Class	10
SR	4-6-2	Battle of Britain Class	40
Total			**1,558**

Left: *This is how locomotives often arrived at a scrapyard after their final journey; as a pair of BR Standard 4MT 4-6-0s have reached Birds Commercial Motors of Long Marston in 1968. The lead engine is thought to be 75047. Note that their coupling rods have been lashed down on those high running plates by the depot staff before their last trip.*
John Fernyhaugh (B304)

Top Right: *Birds' yard was to consume vast numbers of redundant trucks and buses throughout the 1960s and 1970s, but our attention is caught here by BR Standard 4MT 4-6-0 75052. This was ordered in 1953 from Swindon and put in to traffic at the end of 1956. At just 12-years old, it stands in the scrap mound surrounded by an array of discarded locomotive parts. Who can credit that the lightly-engineered Ford 'Y-Type' saloon car probably had a working life of three times longer than the steam engine?*
John Fernyhaugh (B303)

Bottom Right: *After prolonged storage at their former sheds, some engines were deemed as being unfit to travel on the railway network without maintenance to bearings or motion. Therefore several were cut up where they stood, including an unidentified Stanier 8F that has been left as a partially dismembered carcass in the snows of 1968. Three firms are known to have cut engines up at Bolton shed (9K), including Central Wagon, Cox & Danks and T.W. Ward, but we do not know who is responsible for this particular bout of vandalism. No doubt the cutters would return to Bolton to resume their task after the thaw.* Dave Livesey (M503)

The BR build figures per 'Big Four' company design are also interesting: -

Company	Total No. of Classes	Total No Of Locos.
GWR	9	452
LMS	7	640
LNER	6	396
SR	2	50

The striking figure is for the few SR types built, which whilst acknowledging the problems that BR were concerned about with the Bulleid Pacifics, clearly shows that there was already a limited demand for steam locomotives on a railway that had made substantial progress with electrification.

Before World War II, Nigel Gresley had become a big fan of electric traction, and his Woodhead electrification scheme was rapidly re-introduced when peace resumed. Perhaps more careful study back then would have shown this was the best way to modernise the British network?

Nevertheless, the nation was looking for short-term solutions to a long-term problem and the investment that was much needed by the railways had never been forthcoming since the outbreak of World War I. What we had was effectively a bankrupt system begging for state aid, and one that would owe staggering sums by the end of the 1960s (although much of this debt would be eventually written off in the 1968 Transport Act).

Left: *This selection of pictures show what happened to locomotives once they arrived at a private scrapyard, where the disposal process usually took place quite rapidly. In a process not dissimilar to that seen with the 8F at Bolton, this view shows the end of B1 Class 4-6-0 61371. Latterly a resident of March (31B) and previously attending Cambridge (31A) for a number of years, this Thompson locomotive attempts to retain her smokebox number plate to the bitter end. No doubt the men of Cashmores' yard at Great Bridge demolished it at some point in the proceedings of May 1963.* Michael Hale, Trans-Pennine Archive (E393)

Top Right: *At many locations, including Birds and Drapers at Hull (seen here) the dismantlers set up an assembly (or should it be dis-assembly) line to help them ease more engines through the gates of their very busy yards. In this shot we see that the Hull scrapmen have helped another Black Five to bite the dust. It is interesting to note that in this November 1967 visit, the valuable copper fireboxes are left to one side to be reclaimed either by BR or for separate disposal later.* John Gill (M507)

Bottom Right: *After a locomotive was chopped into manageable sized chunks, this is how it all ended up! Chimneys abound in this pile of scrap waiting to be unceremoniously dumped into the 16-ton steel mineral wagon behind the pile in Draper's yard at Hull. The wagon would also become a victim of the scrapmen a few years later on, but one suspects that the waiting B1s would die first.* John Gill (E395)

By 1963 it was obvious to all concerned that the railways were in a terrible mess, both in financial and administrative terms. It had been ten years since they had last made an operating surplus, and after the de-nationalisation of the transport industry by the Conservatives in 1952 it was clear they would never make a profit again.

Progressive freedoms granted to the road haulage and long-distance bus operators meant that integration and rationalisation had been replaced by open competition, despite the fact that the true costs of the road-building programme (and its subsequent repairs) are even now still hidden from the general public. There were also major problems in the dieselisation of the railways, and issues arose concerning the poor reliability of some of the earlier classes that were then coming on stream.

Nevertheless, Beeching took a view that one-third of the railway system carried just one percent of the total rail traffic and that the traffic carried on these routes could easily be transferred to road transport. Be that as it may, what Beeching failed to do was to compare the rail network to a tree, for both have similar characteristics as each has roots, a trunk and branches. If you damage the roots or branches of a physical tree the chances of killing the trunk rise exponentially to the level of pruning.

Beeching's goal was largely a trunk railway system, carrying large volumes of traffic, with the branches eliminated wherever possible. He stated 'the effects of the Re-shaping Plan on the roads will be minimal where it is adverse and substantial where it is beneficial.' Yet, does hindsight show him to have been right?

In the pages that follow, we now begin a representative look at the disposal of the Big Four designs, commencing with the Great Western types that were acquired by BR in 1948, or were continued to be built at Swindon after nationalisation..

Top Left: *A build up of Moguls at Swindon in the late-1950s was beginning to clog the works and occupy valuable storage space, consequently 5393 only stayed a few short months. It was then sent for smelting to the Round Oak Steelworks at Brierley Hill in Staffordshire in February 1960, and our photographer seems to have caught her just before the move on the seventh day of that month.* Frank Hornby (W404)

Top Right: *Three BR-built Castles lead the line at the Coopers Metals' yard, at Sharpness on 22nd August 1964. At this time the yard held at least 15 engines, many minus their tenders, but all of Great Western provenance. At just 15-years old 7015* Carn Brea Castle *leads 7009* Athelney Castle *and 7037* Swindon. *It appears that some of the engines that were sent there may have been moved on and cut elsewhere during the mid-1960s.* Chris Forrest (W783)

Bottom Right: *In contrast this February 1960 view shows 0-6-0PT 1616 minus its chimney (thought to be one of the spark arresting types), whilst it is in company with sister engine 1644 and some Moguls on the scrap lines at Swindon Works. Both are believed to have been broken up here and not sent to private yards for disposal.* Frank Hornby (W399)

The 1962 Transport Act had divorced British Railways from what remained of the rest of the nationalised transport system. Ironically it was soon found that the British Railways Board was then placed in serious competition from its former counterparts within the British Transport Commission, who were by then able to undercut BR's published tariffs and pick off the most lucrative traffic.

Yet, the drastic rationalisation failed to provide a major financial recovery and the BRB deficit for 1963 was £82 million. In accounting terms this was a 21% improvement on the loss of 1962, but when interest charges were added, the deficit for the year was a staggering £134 million. Significantly though, investment in the railways was down substantially to £93 million, compared to £125 million in 1962 and £157 million in 1961.

British Railway's Operating Deficit (in millions)
Before interest and charges applied

1961	1962	1963	1964	1965	1966	1967	1968
£87	£104	£82	£67.5	£73.1	£78.3	£97.4	£87.9

The above figures show that the 'Re-shaping' as a financial argument was not a success, and whilst we know that the trend of heavy losses was reversed by a £56 million surplus in 1969, this would be whittled down to just £11 million after interest and charges were applied. Given that the railways had a debt repayment of £857,110,641 that they would be committed to under the 1962 Act until 1985, the overall trend would continue to range from large losses to very small surpluses year after year.

Left: *Engines large and small have filled the yard at Swindon over the years, as for example the many Broad Gauge types seen after the conversion to 4' 8½" gauge. Some of these were converted in the works, but others were broken up. However, the process was orderly and many parts were salvaged for re-use on other engines. Another old-timer from the start of the 20th century is Churchward 2-8-0 2810, which has been placed in store at the works in October 1959 to await its fate.* Frank Hornby (W330)

Top Right: *By 27th February 1966, this pair of Manor 4-6-0s at Shrewsbury shed ((84G) could have been destined for the scrap. Despite the worst intentions of BR, the pair ended up at Barry. In the longer run 7812* Erlestoke Manor *went to the Severn Valley Railway, whilst the West Somerset Railway provided a home for 7820* Dinmore Manor. J.R. Beddows (W701)

Bottom Right: *Another of those engines that are reputed to have been passed on to Round Oak Steelworks at Brierley Hill was 4201, a Churchward 2-8-0T. It is seen at the end of the line close to C Shop at Swindon Works in February 1960. Inroads into this class had been made in the early 1950s. Despite a period in storage during the 1930s, most of the 100-strong class enjoyed an active life of over 40 years. At Nationalisation all but two of the class (4215 and 4298, which were at St. Blazey in Cornwall) were based at sheds in South Wales. There they performed sterling service on the Welsh Valleys' steeply graded lines, mostly working on coal trains.* Frank Hornby (W302)

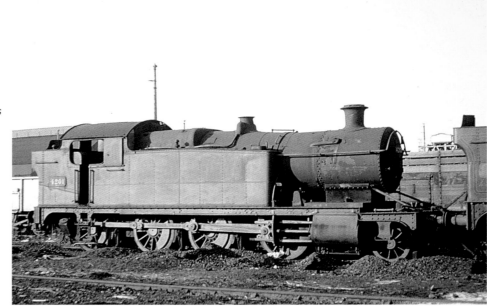

Top Left: *Another class associated with the Welsh coalfield, was the 72xx Class of 1934, which was a Collett re-build of the 42xx Class dating from 1934. One survivor from this class of 2-8-2Ts that would stay at Barry until April 1974 was 7202, which we see on a rainy 12th January 1964. Of the four engines in this picture, she would be purchased by Woodhams, whilst 3689 would go to Birds at Risca a few weeks later. The second Pannier in the line 3748, is destined to go to Swindon to be disposed of! Right at the back is 2-8-2T 7238, which will follow 3689 to the yard at Risca at the end of the year where it would promptly be cut up.* Win Wall, Strathwood Library Collection (W332)

Bottom Left: *One eight-coupled type that is sadly not represented in preservation is the Churchward 47xx 7F 2-8-0 Class. Working fast-fitted freight and parcels trains, but often drawn into relief passenger workings on summer Saturdays, they are sorely missed today. Put out to grass at Swindon in 1962 we find 4702 next to 5906* Lawton Hall, *when their days (and nights) were well and truly numbered.* John Gill (W328)

Top Right: *Found among the dozens of engines in the same visit to Swindon, our contributor has captured 6026* King John *enjoying the company of 5973* Rolleston Hall *as they wait on 'death row' in 1962. One assumes that the King's plates have all been removed for sale, but those from the Hall would have then been less attractive to collectors.* John Gill (W280)

The railways of the 1960s were also faced with the staggering British Railway Board Debt Repayment Schedule, which was sanctioned by the 1962 Transport Act. It called for a repayment of £45,000,000 per annum between January 1965 and January 1969, with £42,000,000 on 1st January 1970. From 1st January 1971 to 1st January 1983 the figure would drop to £40,000,000 each year, then reduce to £35,000,000 on 1st January 1984 and £35,110,641 on 1st January 1985. In total the railways would have to repay the not insignificant sum of £857,110,641.

The debt had been largely incurred by the modernisation programme, of which large sums were squandered on unproven projects. Ironically, the very modern railway that this could have brought about was already being drastically pruned at the same time as it was being improved. Despite the fact that it was known that a large part of BR's assets were to be disposed of before they were anywhere near their life-expectancy, the debt for their acquisition remained and furthermore was subject to a Treasury interest rate of 5.58% per annum.

This added a staggering sum to the principal that was being paid off each year, and in the case of the payment for 1963 (made on 1st July 1964), this was the princely sum of £24,390,660, 13s 0d. This illogical situation continued over the years ahead, and the BRB were paying massive sums in interest on locomotives and rolling stock for 17 years after they had been scrapped.

Basically what the Conservatives did in 1962 was to avoid the issues of properly funding the railways, and pushed the 'notional debt' so far into the future that it would be the responsibility of successive governments for the next 20 to 30 years! The Modernisation Plan therefore became both a futile exercise and a waste of money, with the nation being literally robbed of its investment.

Nowhere was this more clearly demonstrated than in the Standard Class locomotives, many of which were scrapped when only a quarter of the way into their working lives. If you study the pictures in this book and then add this to the reality of the financial position, you cannot but conclude that the wasteful disposal of this valuable asset was quite contrary to good accounting practice.

In total, 13,273 steam engines, many of which had a life expectancy into the 1980s or 1990s, were disposed of in just 92 months (2,751 days). This was an average of nearly five locomotives being scrapped every day, and most of these had many years of working life still ahead of them as the more obsolete members of the BR fleet had been progressively whittled away during the 1950s.

Left: *A refugee from Neath (87A) is found in the lines of engines awaiting disposal at Swindon, this time in the shape of 0-6-0PT 7743. Many of these engines never strayed too far from their home shed, nor enjoyed any glamourous work either. Instead they remained on the books of many a Welsh shed foreman until withdrawal from service. As a consequence many of the class are unlikely to have ever been photographed in black and white let alone colour. Once again this scene is recorded for us in October 1959.*
Frank Hornby (W338)

Top Right: *Remembering the time when you would never be far away from a Pannier Tank on the former Great Western network, this picture emphasises their ubiquitous nature even in death. To followers of other regions they perhaps seemed all the same, because of Swindon's standardisation being applied to the various types. Yet, also of note is just how many outside engine manufacturers built them too! At the head of a long line of them is 9420 trying to prevent an unidentified Castle from escaping the waiting torches in this scene from March 1964 (compare with the view of the same engine shown on page 6).*
Frank Hornby (W242)

Bottom Right: *Echoes of the Great Western Railway lingered right to the very end for 9703, which was one of the condensing-fitted 0-6-0PTs from Old Oak Common. With just a chalked number to confirm its identity at Swindon Works in May 1962, there is no denying her lineage, but by July the scrapmen will have done their worst.*
John Gill (W337)

Top Left: *Despite the fact that this image has not suffered the ravages of time very well, it is worthy of inclusion because it shows that Swindon's dump seems to have become cluttered again by April of 1965, but this time with the remains of deceased Pannier tank boilers. Right up until closure, visitors to the works could always find the carcasses of locomotives at this point, even if they were diesels. Visits to the works will be covered in greater detail for both eras in upcoming volumes.*
Edward Dorricott (W400)

Bottom Left: *Not all of the ex GWR or BR locos that made it to Barry would survive, but one that has clung on (just) is Castle Class 7027 Thornbury Castle. Built in 1949 at Swindon she lasted just 15 years in BR service and is pictured in 1969. Best described as a long-term project, and with no date set currently for its restoration, this engine now has been out of use for 40 years. Note the condemned wagons in the background, which are pressed into service to hold sleepers.*
J.R. Beddows (W306)

Top Right: *Considering just how long many of the Barry engines sat out on the edge of docks (in rain, salt air and baking sun), it is amazing to note just how many have survived. One engine to only just make it to the hands of the preservationists is 3862, one of the Collett versions of the 28xx Class of 2-8-0s, built during the dark days of World War II. Once again back on 26th January 1968, consideration of it still being around in any form by the millennium was fanciful folly.*
J.R. Beddows (W260)

Looking at the number of locomotives that were permanently taken out of service during the 1960s shows the extent of the scrapping work that followed: -

1961	1962	1963	1964	1965	1966	1967	1968
1,581	2,924	1,762	2,075	1,987	1,298	1,329	359

The scale of the operation now assumes momentous proportions, and when the numbers of scrapped locomotives are multiplied by their individual tonnage the figures seem astronomical.

The answer is pure maths, but the calculations for the 999 BR Standards alone would be a mammoth task. Take for example the Standard 2MT 2-6-0 locomotive, which weighed 49-tons 5-cwt for the engine and 36-ton 17-cwt for the tender, so the scrap weight of 65 engines was 5,720-tons.

Imagine then the total weight of the 9F 2-10-0s, where the locomotives alone weighed 86-tons 14-cwt or 90-tons 4-cwt for a Crosti-boilered version? Returning to our chosen example class, the Britannia Pacifics, the 53 engines that went for scrap yielded no less than 4,982-tons and that did not include the tenders.

Even the real lightweights of steam, say for example the ten ex-LNER Y3 Class Sentinel 0-4-0Ts that were in Departmental Stock in 1959, would contribute 207.5-tons of scrap. The 666-strong 8F fleet of 1959 would amount to nearly half-a-million tons without their tenders. The 258 Hall Class 4-6-0s on 1959 would make nearly a third-of-a-million tons of scrap when their tenders were weighed in as well. This is a rough measure, but it illustrates the idea!

Now follows the question, how did they break the engines? The answer is simple, it was by means of hard manual labour that was both dirty and dangerous. In previous works on this subject I estimated that the breaking of 16,108 locomotives took about 1.28 million man hours; this being based on the fact that an average locomotive could be broken in a week.

Some of the people involved in the scrap industry say that this may have been a fair estimate in the larger more efficient yards, but the smaller ones took considerably longer. Based on this information, we looked at the figures once again, and estimated that perhaps a figure of 1.5 million man hours might be more appropriate - nearly all of it being spent outdoors in all weathers.

The tools the scrapmen had at their disposal were nothing more than primitive; axes, sledgehammers, chisels and oxy-acetylene cutting gear. Their task with these tools was to reduce anything from an 0-4-0 to a 2-10-0 into uniform chunks of scrap. To fit into the scrap metal pans at the steel smelting mills, the overall size was normally a maximum of 5' x 1' 6" (1.52m x 0.46m). Imagine into just how many slices the frames of a Britannia Pacific would have to be cut? The traditional British locomotive frames used 1" (25mm) or 1½" (38mm) rolled steel plate. Even this was considered to be lightweight, as they were prone to suffer fatigues or cracks in service. However, when bar frames were considered for the Standards, the railway workshops did not have the facilities to produce them.

Left: *In a pair of pictures showing how steam locomotives were dismembered, we have another rare view of Willoughby's yard at Choppington. Next in the line to be cut up is J27 0-6-0 65842, while the executioners finish off their work on an ex-WD 2-8-0 on 21st January 1967. From this and several other views, it can be seen that locomotive fireboxes were often left intact. However, it is academic on these war-time engines as the fireboxes were made of steel to save valuable resources.*
John Gleen (E382)

Right: *This scene on 5th January 1965 is one that would horrify any safety or insurance consultant today, as the asbestos has been crudely hacked off the boiler barrels on 4082 Windsor Castle. This is just three days after the engine's arrival in the small yard of Cox & Danks at Park Royal, as work moves rapidly ahead without any consideration of the fact that a visitor with a camera could record the dangerous scene. Furthermore, the victim being despatched without ceremony is what was once regarded as a 'Royal' engine. King George VI had once taken the controls of Windsor Castle, but at the time of his funeral the engine was in the works at Swindon. As a result the funeral train was hauled by 7013 Bristol Castle carrying the nameplates from Windsor Castle, a switch that was never corrected afterwards. Not for the first time was such a crafty switch of identity made to save face. A legend persists amongst those involved in the cutting up process, as they swear that a pre-war Castle took longer to cut up, as the steel was of a better quality than that of a later build.*
Aldo Delicata (W271)

Top Left: *Staying with the thought of unsafe working practices, asbestos litters the environment as 8F 2-8-0 48469 receives the attention of two cutters. They appear to be attacking all the seams and original joints where possible, as these would be the weakest points. They are most likely to be on piecework whilst engaged on cutting duties at Bolton shed on 30th January 1968.*
J.R. Beddows (M464)

Bottom Left: *One would assume that Swindon Works have perfected the art of cutting up by the time Collett 0-6-2T 5682 was observed in the course of demolition on 12th August 1962. Although there is evidence of pre-cutting along the bottom of the tank rivet lines, the cab has gone as have the studs holding the buffers in place. We cannot guess the reason for the small oblong cut on the smokebox where the top lamp bracket would have been, unless it was to relieve the boredom of spending all your working days cutting up engines. Now who fancies a smokebox plate for a few bob then?*
Frank Hornby (W287)

Top Right: *Although most of the backhead fittings have gone in this view at Barry in 1967, many other useful and valuable pieces remain in place even though the engine will have been a resident in the yard for a couple of years already. Lubricators, injectors, and even the driver's drop down wooden seat still survive. Before engines started to escape there was no need to shunt the hulks, therefore ex-GWR specimens are found as far as the eye can see.* Win Wall;
Strathwood Library Collection (W235)

The task of cutting a Britannia into slices was hard enough, especially when you consider it was 68' 9" (21m) long over the buffers. Most of the engine's make up was from ferrous metal, and the complicated task of breaking a locomotive was not always compensated for by the going price of scrap. A classic example of this is found in the case of Woodham Brothers, Barry, who found it more profitable to cut up railway mineral wagons and brake vans rather than the 220+ locomotives they had sitting there awaiting disposal.

The Barry story of course is unique in the history of the World's railways, and the very simple economics of locomotive disposal and the price of scrap ensured so many hulks would be sold for preservation and not melted down!

Of course the real prize was the non-ferrous metal contents, predominantly the backhead fittings and the firebox. On a Britannia the firebox measured 7' 0" (2.14m) by 7' 9" (2.36m), about 273 cubic feet in all. Copper was used for the inner fireboxes of all the BR Standards, in line with GWR and LMS practice. The American argument for using steel fireboxes was discounted (despite the lightness and cheapness of construction), as these types were very dependent on properly treated water supplies.

The durable copper boxes were much more resistant to corrosion and less likely to suffer from cracking or failure. The result was a higher construction cost, but also a far greater scrap value, especially if BR did not specify the return of the firebox as a condition of the sale.

If a private scrap merchant bought the engine in its entirety, the price would generally be around £1,250 to £1,400 higher, but as a scrapyard could obtain upwards of £2,000 for a firebox, it was worth the extra cost. Oddly BR did not always bother to reclaim the firebox it had retained title to, and I can recall seeing lines of neatly stacked fireboxes awaiting collection by BR at many scrapyards in the period concerned.

One Scottish breaker confided in me that they had scrapped about 35 locomotives where the fireboxes were not included in the sale, but these had never been collected by BR, despite written and telephoned requests. When the yard went over to diesel work in 1969, the fireboxes were sold for £54,500 so they could free up the needed space, but despite telling BR they never claimed the money.

The BR fitters did have a habit of removing all the backhead fittings however, usually before an engine was moved from its last shed into a disposal line or dump. This was done to prevent petty thievery, as such items were easily removed and almost as good as church roof lead for ready cash. The loss of these fittings has of course been so detrimental to many of the preservation schemes that have followed over the years, but they were logical at the time.

The rest of the locomotive was a mixture of steel, cast-iron and both ferrous and non-ferrous tubing. The trouble is that the locomotives also contained a large quantity of substances hazardous to health. First of all, there were large quantities of oil and grease, most of which would be burned off before work began on dismantling. Next came the ash, sludge and coal that had often been left on the engine.

Left: *From this view at Cohen's Yard at Cransley near Kettering the reader might be forgiven for thinking they were south of the Thames. Not only did this firm break a large number of steam locomotives, but they also scrapped a lot of the redundant London Transport 1927 series tube stock. Several Southern Region engines also went here and one such example is this ex-LSWR S15 4-6-0 30507, which still has its tender filled with coal from its home shed of Feltham (70B). It was withdrawn at Christmas 1963, and ventured north in March 1964 for a quick exit.* Win Wall; Strathwood Library Collection (S303)

Top Right: *Withdrawn on 8th June 1963 34035* Shaftesbury *is still at the Eastleigh Works in November that year. With a credited mileage of 764,306 to show for her 17-years service, this engine was scrapped in the week ending 25th January 1964. Cut up at the same time was 34074 46* Squadron, *but with even less miles on the clock she is perhaps the rarest of all Bulleids filmed in colour, unless you know better?* The late Norman Browne; Strathwood Library Collection (S207)

Bottom Right: *Few members of the King Arthur Class are seen in colour pictures as the first of these, 30754* The Green Knight, *was scrapped in 1953. By the time that 30794* Sir Ector de Maris *was making its departure in September 1960, most of the class had already vanished, mainly at Eastleigh and Brighton works but even Ashford claimed one for scrapping. Now reduced to just the frames it is easy to see why some engines perhaps were never the same again after a crash.* Strathwood Library Collection (S201)

However, most hazardous of all was the copious levels of asbestos that had been used as boiler lagging and the like. The men would have to remove this, usually by hand and few of them had any form of respiratory protection.

Today an example of the toxicity of this material is found at the site of the Darlington Works under a tract of grassland alongside the town's North Road Railway Museum! On that site steam locomotives had been cut up over the years, and the asbestos became impregnated in the sub-soil. In February 2003, Darlington Borough Council published its *Contaminated Land Inspection Strategy*, which looked (in part) at the issues facing the authority over the North Road site almost four decades after steam locomotive scrapping came to an end at the works in March 1964.

Even so, the bulk of the material was taken away in the 1950s and '60s and dumped in the Civil Engineer's tip at Witton Park near Bishop Auckland. The contamination was of course buried under tons of spoil and ballast, but nobody will ever know how much still lurks down there!

Few of the manual workers engaged in the disposal of the British steam locomotive fleet, either at the BR works or private yards, ever had the protection of today's Health & Safety Executive regulations, especially COSHH. They were relatively well-paid, but not excessively so. Injuries such as bad cuts, broken limbs, crushed feet and hands were all commonplace, and I have been able to trace some fatal incidents. Yet as the reader will appreciate, this is not a subject that anyone wants to talk about after so many years.

Left: *Three of the 40-strong Schools Class were to be fortunate enough to make it into preservation; 30925* Repton *managing it via a time in the USA. In the case of 30921* Shrewsbury *seen at Cohen's of Cransley in May 1964, someone seems to have been a bit confused. Chalked on the place where her nameplate was once mounted, someone has written the name Guildford.*
Win Wall, Strathwood Library Collection (S208)

Top Right: *Built to an original design of Urie, H15 Class 4-6-0 30482 saw many modifcations after 1914. Its mileage record shows it had managed a credible 1,471,917 miles in traffic when it was withdrawn in May 1959. It then spent around 12 weeks at Eastleigh, first on the shed and then in the works, before finally being reduced to piles of scrap metal in August 1959.*
 Trans-Pennine Archive (S651)

Bottom Right: *With Schools Class 4-6-0 30900* Eton *just behind her this Stroudley E6 0-6-2T has just arrived at Ashford Works for disposal from the temporary store that was built up at Feltham (70B). Considering the number of engines that passed through these works for both repair and scrapping, Ashford rarely appears in colour pictures. Despite being in the 'Garden of England', this view from February 1962 shows decidedly poor weather conditions, as sleet falls on the waiting victims. We of course would be delighted to hear from anyone who photographed at the works in better conditions.*
Strathwood Library Collection (S222)

Top Left: *In November 1963 Eastleigh Works was getting through its scrapping quotas quite smartly. For example 31919, a Maunsell W Class 2-6-4T from Norwood Junction (75C) was withdrawn and scrapped in the same month. Nine of the 15-strong class passed through Eastleigh in rapid succession about this time; with Cohen's at Cransley bagging four and Birds of Morriston picking up a brace.*
The late Norman Browne;
Strathwood Library Collection (S173)

Bottom Left: *Once Eastleigh Works gave up scrapping engines, its 'disposals' were sent to Salisbury or Gloucester as a means of getting them closer to the scrapyards of South Wales. However those cripples too sick to make the journey often received the attention of Cohen's men who travelled to cut them at various sheds. This view at Eastleigh works yard in March 1966 shows all that is left of N Class mogul 31866. Standing ominously behind with a sack over the chimney is 30925 Repton, awaiting restoration and shipping across the Atlantic.*
Len Smith (S181)

Top Right: *The Slag Reduction Company, of Ickles in Rotherham took serious steps to keep unwanted visitors at bay. Here we witness the arrival of U Class Mogul 31793 from Guildford (70C), in a view that shows the 'Stalag' type compound erected to protect the firm's new investments. Many yards also kept large, hairy and ferocious Alsatians to dissuade unwanted visitors after dark. This particular shot would have been taken around Christmas of 1964.*
Trans-Pennine Archive (S220)

As stated, the bulk of the scrapping work was undertaken outdoors, even in the dead of winter, when ice and snow made cutting work especially hazardous. However, work often continued thanks to the supplies of coal that were left in a locomotive's tender or bunker, and this would be raked out and dumped in piles around the engine. When set alight, often by using the cutting gear to start the conflagration, the glowing heaps of coal provided some respite from the searing British weather.

The teams of men, usually three or four per engine, would set to work and the demolition process began. Yet, visiting enthusiasts could usually manage to acquire a builder's plate or the like for the price of a pint!

Nameplates were another matter, and few of these went to the scrapyard. For example, the Britannia Class had their names removed long before their final days of service. The exception was of course those locomotives that had names painted on their splashers (as for example many of the Scottish types) and these would be cut off rather crudely in the BR works. A bothy at the Inverurie Works in Aberdeenshire had its walls covered with such examples, but some slipped into the hands of private owners. Loco lamps were more readily available, and I still have one or two in my garage that were acquired for about five shillings (25p) each. However, most of my scrapyard trophies and I parted company years ago in a time of financial hardship!

The rapid end for most engines saw very little being saved in the way of souvenirs, as the yards worked with ruthless efficiency. Originally the scrapping was mostly undertaken in BR Works, but as the pace of the withdrawals accelerated, they were simply unable to cope.

Not only that, but the Workshops were also under the watchful eye of their political masters, and it was secretly held that once steam-building had finished, construction work could be more competitively handled by tender from private firms.

Under a general heading of the *British Railways Workshops Plan*, published in September 1962, a central management was formed to reach certain objectives. Its wording perhaps typical of the BBC series *Yes Minister*.

"To achieve the rationalisation for existing rolling stock construction and repair facilities to cater economically for future planned commitments, the redevelopment and re-equipment in accordance with more modern practice of those Works which were to continue, and the streamlining of the labour force to match these radical changes." In other words, it was a plan to modernise a token few and shut the rest down.

However, in practice it was not quite so easy to achieve this all at once, but the BRB's 1963 Annual Report stated:-

"Full advantage has been taken of the rapid rundown in the use of steam traction and of the concentration of the maintenance and repair of specific rolling stock types at particular Works to reduce the holding of spares.....!"

Left: *Arriving at the familiar yard of Woodhams in May 1965 Battle of Britain Class 34070* Manston *looks to be in reasonable condition. These shots from the 1960s are a marked contrast to the ugliness of the views taken a decade later. As locos became parted from their tenders, cladding was also crudely removed to allow the boilers to be painted to help protect them from further corrosion. Then of course there were the slogans showing how each engine was reserved for one of the new preservation schemes that were then popping up all over.* Trans-Pennine Archive (S240)

Top Right: *Still showing the different lining pattern for the high sided tenders on Bulleid engines three years after arriving at Barry, is 34072 257* Squadron. *We have mused elsewhere on the outcome of the Barry yard miracle, and how different things might have been if it had occurred in one of the other major yards. Say it had been McWilliams yard at Shettleston, perhaps our preserved lines would have had a fleet of Britannia Pacifics, and then some of the class would have been able to live up to their expected working lives after all!* John Gill (S209)

Bottom Right: *A pair of withdrawn Merchant Navy Pacifics both went to Slag Reduction from the early withdrawals of this class at the end of 1964! These were 35002* Union Castle *(seen here), and 35015* Rotterdam Lloyd. *The fact that Rotherham was so far from their original operating area, aroused much interest amongst local enthusiasts, some of whom travelled from all over the Midlands and the north to catch a glimpse of these two unusual victims.* Trans-Pennine Archive (S223)

The centralisation of workshop management under the Derby Works called for a reduction of main works from 28 to 16, and in sheet works from 12 to five. Further economies were made by the reductions in the numbers of iron foundries, spring shops, hot forging shops and brass foundries. For example, the brass foundries were reduced from 15 to just four and those that survived were expected to compete with one another.

The year 1963 saw the closures of the works at:

Ashford Loco Works	Nine Elms Sheet Works
Caerphilly Works	St. Helens Sheet Works
Faverdale Works	Stratford Works
Gorton Works	Walker Gate Carriage Works
Manchester Sheet Works	Trent Sheet Works
Newhaven Sheet Works	York Wagon Works

In addition, 'progress' was made in centralising repair work to specific workshops, and steam locomotive work was discontinued at Derby, Doncaster and St. Rollox, with the same planned for Horwich and Wolverhampton in 1964. The scrapping of steam locomotives was now very much considered as an outside activity, and having been started on the Western Region in 1959, it was already in full swing.

Our previous book, *Steam For Sale* has already discussed how the move into private scrapping began, so we do not propose to cover the same ground here. However, we must acknowledge the fact, that with the diminishing capacity of the railway workshops and the centralisation of management and specialisation of the works, it would have been impossible for most BR plants to continue scrapping for very long after the 1962-64 changes.

Left: *Inverurie Works came under plans for closure as part of the* Re-shaping of British Railways. *However, the resulting unemployed workforce would not be easily taken up by other local industries in this remote part of North-East Scotland; aside from farming and the production of whisky there was little alternative work for men trained in heavy engineering. Therefore to help prolong the painful closure process many locomotives were sent north for disposal. However not all of those engines destined for Inverurie seem to have been cut up at the works after all. Here 40661, a Class 2P 4-4-0 waits transfer from Inverurie in 1961! Even so published records show her as being stored at Kilmarnock Works until she passed to Connell's at Calder for cutting in July of 1963.* Frank Hornby (M510)

Top Right: *One of the Fairburn designed 2-6-4Ts to find their way to a cold and bitter end at the hands of Drapers men in Hull was 42296. Seen here in the snows of January 1966, she has been dragged across the Pennines from Lostock Hall (10D) where she would have been in the company of designs from both Stanier and Ivatt.* John Gill (M465)

Bottom Right: *An engine on which I had several cab rides along the Meltham branch was 42863, when it was allocated to Huddersfield Hillhouse (55G). It was later transferred to Ayr (67C), where we see the Hughes 6P5F 'stored' in 1966. Highly regarded by enginemen these powerful locomotives would be sorely missed by Ayr's footplatemen after steam finished there on the 9th December 1966.* Douglas Paul (M434)

Top Left: *Considering just how many scrapyards were located around England's 'Steel City' (Sheffield) it is surprising how little colour material is available to show the carnage these yards wreaked with the British Railways steam fleet! Three of H.G. Ivatt's moguls (43157, 43059 and 43085) wait their turn outside Thos. Ward's yard at Killamarsh on 14th March 1965. They would have made a short trip from nearby Staveley/Barrow Hill (41E) where they had sat for a couple of months. Even so Messer's Wards had obviously acted promptly when the chance to tender for their purchase was made. Win Wall, Strathwood Library Collection (M416)*

Bottom Left: *On the same visit our photographer bagged a pair of chimney-less Fowler 4F 0-6-0s, the lead engine 44497 being from Buxton (9L). It is quite possible that the chimneys had been removed for sale as souvenirs; they made great flowerpots! Win Wall, Strathwood Library Collection (M417)*

Top Right: *Fortunately 46243 City of Lancaster still has its double chimney in place, but for how much longer? We find the former WCML regular in the Central Wagon Works at Ince, Wigan on 2nd May 1965. Records show her as being withdrawn from Camden (1B) during the week ending 12th September 1964, but she had already seen three periods in store prior to this. Ignoring the costs of repairs etc her final recorded mileage of 1,526,292 miles can be set against her construction costs of £10,838 (including the original tender), making for less than a penny a mile capital cost. Win Wall, Strathwood Library Collection (M439)*

Let us consider then the cessation of the scrapping at BR Works. In the ex-GWR plants, the end of scrapping, according to the Annual Reports are as follows; Barry 1958, Caerphilly 1962, Swindon 1965 and Wolverhampton 1964.

At the former Southern Railway workshops it was Ashford 1963, Brighton 1958, Eastleigh 1964 (and whilst cutting continued there, it was by private contractors), followed by Ryde or Newport on the Isle of Wight where the last work was carried out on the O2 class in 1967.

As for the ex-LMS works, the story was much the same and the order was, Crewe 1965, Derby 1963, Horwich 1964, Kilmarnock 1959, St. Rollox 1964 and Wolverton (carriages) 1959. The LNER works lasted longer, but finally went like this; Cowlairs 1964, Darlington 1964, Doncaster 1964, Inverurie 1963, Gorton 1963 and Stratford in 1961.

The cut-back in scrapping at the BR Works was therefore more closely tied in with the implementation of the *British Railways Workshops Plan*, than my original research had originally given credit.

This new volume does not intend to re-hash the work of the original three volumes, nor the work of *Steam For Scrap - The Complete Story*, although the reader would be advised to study those volumes alongside these new books. These earlier volumes (although now out of print) looked at the workshops and scrapyards in detail, along with accounts about how dumps appeared, the road to the scrapyard, dead engine movements, and so on. They then went on to look at specific locomotive classes (as for example the Giants of Steam) and then considered the various private scrapyards. Our remit is somewhat different!

Above: *Already missing her smokebox door, Jinty 0-6-0T 47396 is sandwiched with her fellow works shunters from Wolverton, when seen here in the Northamptonshire yard of Cohen's at Cransley in April 1967.*
John Gill (M414)

Of course it was the private scrapyards that became an important part of the story during the last five years of steam disposal. However, whilst the bulk of steam locomotives were cut up and gone by 1969, the distinction of being the last BR steam engines to go into the melting pot fell to GWR Pannier 4156 and BR Standard 9F 2-10-0 92085, which were finally broken up at Woodham's yard in the summer of 1980 as they were too far gone to be considered as realistic preservation projects.

The list right shows all the firms who are known to have purchased locomotives from British Railways, the ones in bold text were the major operations where locomotives were purchased in their hundreds.

Some yards, on the other hand bought only one locomotive, and this would include the firm of L.C. Hughes who acquired one GWR 0-6-0 for its yard at Port Talbot, but according to several readers never completely cut up the engine and finally sold it to Cox & Danks. In total around 50 to 60 small yards existed, cutting up no more than a handful of engines each, but even now it is obvious that we have not tracked down all the purchasers. Several firms in Nottinghamshire are thought to have bought locomotives, and the same is true of scrap yards in the West Midlands and Lancashire.

The Private Scrapyards That Purchased British Railways Steam Engines By Tender

Scrapyard	Location
Ardmore Steels	Craigendoran
Armitage & Son	Sheepbridge
Arnott & Young	Bradford
Arnott & Young	Bilston
Arnott & Young	Carmyle
Arnott & Young	Dinsdale
Arnott & Young	Glasgow
Arnott & Young	Parkgate
Arnott & Young	Troon
Barlborough Metals	Briton Ferry
Barlborough Metals	Lanelly
Barnes & Bell	Coatbridge
M Baum	Middlesbro'
Birds Group	Lanelly
Birds Group	Long Marston
Birds Group	Morriston
Birds Group	Newport
Birds Group	Risca
T. Burton	Middleton
Bush & Sons	Pye Bridge
G W Butler	Bradford
G W Butler	Otley
J Buttigieg	Pontnewydd
J Buttigieg	Newport
G H Campbell	Airdrie
G H Campbell	Shieldhall
Carrex Metals	Rochdale
J Cashmore	Great Bridge
J Cashmore	Newport
Central Wagon	Wigan
Central Wagon	Barrow
Clayton & Davie	Gateshead
G Cohen	Cargo Fleet
G Cohen	Kettering
G Cohen	Morriston
G Cohen	Rotherwas
J N Connell	Coatbridge
Coopers Metals	Sharpness
Cox & Danks	Barry
Cox & Danks	Cardiff
Cox & Danks	Manchester
Cox & Danks	North Acton
Cox & Danks	Park Royal
Cox & Danks	Sheffield
Cox & Danks	Warley
Crump & Sons	Flint
A Draper	Hull
Ellis Metals	Blaydon
J Friswell	Banbury
W George	Wath
R S Hayes	Bridgend
Hayes Metals	Gloucester
Walter Hesslewood	Sheffield
Hendersons	Airdrie
Holinter	Grays
L C Hughes	Port Talbot
Hughes Bolckows	North Blyth
T Jenkins	Port Talbot
H & B Jolliffe	Newport IoW
T H Jones	Newport
A King & Son	Norwich
A Loom (Ellis Metals)	Spondon
P & W McLellan	Bo'Ness
P & W McLellan	Langloan
J McWilliam	Shettleston
Madden & McKee	Bootle
J Mahoney	Newport
Marple & Gillott	Attercliffe
Mayer & Newman	Blackwall
I & R Morkott	Caerphilly
Motherwell Machinery	Wishaw
T L Mumford	Plaistow
C Murphy	Liverpool
North Wales Wagon	Chester
J & S Parker	Altrincham
Rigley's Wagon Works	Nottingham
Round Oak Steel Works	Brierley Hill
Slag Reduction Co.	Barrow
Slag Reduction Co.	Briton Ferry
Slag Reduction Co.	Swansea
Slag Reduction Co.	Rotherham
Settle Speakman	Queenborough
Ship Breaking Ind's	Helensburgh
Slater Bros	Attercliffe
W F Smith	Sheffield
Steel Breaking	Chesterfield
Steel Supply	Briton Ferry
Steel Supply	Swansea
Steel Supply	West Drayton
Taylor Bros	Manchester
T J Thompson	Stockton
R S Tyley	Barry
D. Ward & Co	Burton
T W Ward	Barrow
T W Ward	Beighton
T W Ward	Briton Ferry
T W Ward	Broughton La
T W Ward	Darlington
T W Ward	Grays
T W Ward	Inverkeithing
T W Ward	Killamarsh
T W Ward	Manchester
T W Ward	Mexborough
T W Ward	Middlesbro'
T W Ward	Mostyn
T W Ward	Preston
T W Ward	Ringwood
T W Ward	Wishaw
West Scotland Ship	Troon
W Willoughby	Choppington
P Wood	Lancaster
Peter Woods	Rotherham
I C Woodfield	Cadoxton
I C Woodfield	Newport
Woodfield & Way	Cardiff
Woodfield & Way	Newport
Woodham Brothers	Barry

Top Left: *Crewe Works used a variety of 0-6-0 types from the Midland, Furness, Lancashire & Yorkshire and of course the LNWR as works shunters. By the early 1960s these pre-Grouping types were in fast decline, but it seems that very little colour photography exists of Crewe Works actually breaking up engines. This is most likely due to the fact that most were broken inside the workshops and film speeds in colour were frighteningly low. We are perhaps fortunate then to see a shot of one of the rebuilt G2A stalwarts, 49129, making her last curtain call at the works.* Richard Sinclair Collection (M435)

Bottom Left: *One piece of good fortune was the arrival of two of the ex Somerset & Dorset Joint Railway 2-8-0s into the sanctuary of Woodhams. Whilst one of the previously mentioned G2As was saved as part of the National Collection, the preservation of examples from all the pre-Grouping concerns was sadly not part of the plan. Seen here after a light shower in August 1964 the 7F still looks to be in pretty good condition.* Win Wall, Strathwood Library Collection (M454)

Top Right: *Perhaps the only redeeming factor in seeing a locomotive being cut up in this manner is the fact that it affords the chance to see how they were constructed and the gauge of materials used. An unidentified Stanier 8F demonstrates some of the building techniques while she is undressed. Sections of other victims and her tender lie all about, with the ever-present cylinders to fuel the torches never far away in this April 1967 scene at Cohen's scrapyard in Cransley.* John Gill (M432)

At this stage in history we will have difficulties in tracing all the missing yards, unless of course readers can provide categoric proof in the shape of photographs or written records. A few years ago we were contacted by a former Director of Thomas W. Ward who said that he still had all the firm's disposal records in his loft, but couldn't access them as he was in the process of converting his property; other scrap company records turned up in Turkey!

For most of these operations, the disposal of a steam locomotive was not a case of sentimentality or even basic record-keeping; the objective was to turn a redundant piece of machinery into saleable scrap metal as quickly as possible. Some of the scrapyards allowed visitors, others actively discouraged them, so photographing the end of steam was rather like some kind of lottery, and one with not very favourable odds at that.

To discuss the activities of the major yards would be a physical impossibility for a number of factors, but we cannot ignore two or three important locations, the first of which has to be the two yards of John Cashmore Limited, which were located at Great Bridge in Tipton, Staffordshire and at Newport in Monmouthshire.

Both began their work in 1959, although Great Bridge started not with engines, but rather with EMUs following the cessation of carriage scrapping at Wolverton Works. It was not until the end of the year that 4-4-0 2Ps arrived for breaking, with 40553/87 and 40675. These were rapidly followed by 3-cylinder 4-4-0 4Ps 41083, 41113/22, which came from one of the dumps outside Derby. Early in 1960, the Dump at Winsford supplied ex-LNWR G2a 0-8-0s and LT&SR tanks that had been held in store there. It was the start of a massive slaughter of around 1,250 engines.

The firm's Newport yard, conveniently situated for the South Wales' smelting mills, handled well over 1,000 steam engines in a ten-year period from the end of 1959. That meant an aggregate of no less than 100 steam engines per annum, near enough two a week. Situated on what had been the Western Dry Dock, the yard dealt with its steady progression of victims, many of which (490) were of GWR origin.

Newport started with a quartet of Churchward 2-8-0s from Swindon in April 1959 (2808/10/24/26) and took whatever it was offered thereafter. This included no less than four King Class, 37 Castle Class, 13 County Class, 51 Hall Class, 20 Modified Hall Class, 12 Grange Class, three Manor Class, 34 Moguls and 43 ex-SR Bulleid Pacifics. The yard also gobbled up 165 BR Standards, and the Britannias 70017 *Arrow* and 70026 *Polar Star*.

Left: *Gresley 60026* Miles Beevor *became a parts donor for two of the preserved A4s,* 60007 Sir Nigel Gresley *and* 60008 Dwight D. Eisenhower. *Stabled alongside it at Crewe Works for many weeks was the unique* 71000 Duke of Gloucester, *which was only initially due to have just the cylinders and valve gear preserved; thankfully it later passed to Barry from where it was saved. However, 60026 was sent to Hughes Bolckow's yard in Morpeth for final demolition.*
D Lewis, S Carter Collection (E383)

Top Right: *Following the misfortunes of Gresley Pacifics we find A3 60098* Spion Kop *(named after the 1920 Derby winner) going to the 'knackers yard' at Inverurie Works in November 1963. This was just a few months after 60103 Flying Scotsman had passed to the care of Alan Peglar, for whose brave financial venture we are all grateful. Without this leap of faith the preservation world would undoubtedly have evolved very differently. It was a demonstration of the fact that one man or a small group of enthusiasts could club together and purchase their own engine.*
Douglas Paul (E384)

Bottom Right: *A number of very small scrap yards in the North East accounted for several engines, most being from local sheds. As a consequence, activities at yards like Clayton & Davis at Dunston-on-Tyne or Willoughby's of Chopington were not widely recorded and photography was rare. Among these victims was Q6 0-8-0 63440, whilst another of her class already reduced to its frames lies behind when this photograph was taken on 17th January 1967.* Douglas Paul (E394)

Having considered the two major yards, we now take a look at the other big names in the disposal of steam, commencing with Arnott & Young Ltd. This was a firm with a number of scrapping locations, including the long-established West of Scotland Ship Breaking Co. Ltd. of Troon in Ayrshire that they acquired in the early-1960s.

Arnott & Young's biggest operation in England was at Parkgate & Rawmarsh near Rotherham, which was very close to the Aldwalke Steel Works, but very cramped and limited to two or three locomotives at a time. Around 70 or so steam engines were cut up there, including a fair number of WD 8F 2-8-0s, BR Standard 9Fs and LNER 04s. Also dismantled were two named B1s from Wakefield and the Staveley Steel Works shunters.

At the West of Scotland yard, the company succeeded in breaking no less than eight LMS Duchess Class Pacifics, coming third behind Crewe Works (17 engines) and Cashmore's Great Bridge (nine engines). It also took one Britannia, 70019 *Lightning*. The firm's yard at Carmyle had nine A3s from Scottish sheds, and also took a long-time favourite of mine D11 Class 62418 *The Pirate*, which I had photographed a few times at Thornton Junction.

The Birds Group came relatively late into the scrapping of steam engines, around 1964, but its yard at Risca in Monmouthshire assumed significant proportions as it handled approaching 200 steam locomotives, not 172 as erroneously suggested in the earlier books. We now know that no less than 162 of these were of GWR origin and 23 were BR Standards, (figures quoted in the first three volumes of the *Steam For Scrap* books, which gave a total of 185). Add to this two SR S15s, four smaller ex-SR types and half a dozen LMS engines and the figure becomes more complete. By the end of 1967, it seems that Birds were directing purchases to either their yard at Long Marston or the yard of R. S. Hayes in Bridgend, which the company had purchased in 1965.

The firm's other yards all handled a substantial number of steam engines, but it seems to have been company policy to move the work around; possibly to reduce the distance that dead engines had to travel. One of the firm's busy yards, that at Morriston near Swansea saw a significant fall off in acquisitions in 1967.

Morriston had handled a significant number of engines, mostly GWR types and BR Standards, of which it broke 83 and 20 respectively. The Bridgend yard had handled 233 GWR engines whilst in the ownership of R. S. Hayes, and then taken a further 46 after it was acquired by Birds. As a whole, the group broke a large number of the 'Giants of Steam' including King Class 6028 (Risca), Merchant Navy Class 35016 and 35021 (Bridgend) and no less than 18 West Country/Battle of Britain Light Pacifics (nine at Llanelly, six at Bridgend and three at Morriston).

One of the big disposal areas was Newport in Monmouthshire, and this was the location of J. Buttigieg Ltd., although it seems likely that they first commenced loco-breaking at Pontnewydd. They seemed to have had a voracious appetite for GWR classes, but they also got their teeth into no less than 18 ex-SR Light Pacifics and six Merchant Navy Pacifics. A figure of between 45 and 48 BR Standards went there as well. Total figures are not known for this company, but the records for 1966 showed that 122 engines were cut up in that year alone.

Another of the big scrapping areas was found in Central Scotland, as yards there were feeding the steel mills in Lanarkshire with scrap. The firm of G. H. Campbell were known to operate from two main yards, one in Airdrie, Lanarkshire, the other was at Shieldhall in Renfrewshire. However, anecdotal evidence shows that they may have worked at other locations, including BR sheds, redundant goods yards and at some of the small dumps. Their earliest purchases came from dumps around Manchester and from Gorton Works and had some unlikely candidates, including ex-GCR, ex-LNW, ex-MR and ex-L&YR engines.

Stanier engines then began to appear in substantial numbers and included here were 2-6-2T, Jubilee, Black Five, and 8F class members. As LNER-built locomotives became 'surplus' in Scotland, the firm took its share but it was the two A2 Class 60529 and 60534, and the three A4 Class members, 60005, 60027 and 60031 that will be most sorely missed. Several BR Standards, including 9Fs and ten Britannias were demolished, before the company turned its attention to the early diesel locomotives that had been allocated to the Scottish Region and failed to perform anything like satisfactorily.

I have previously stated that some of the private scrapyards have, despite repeated attempts, proved to be something of a mystery, and a classic example of this is the Central Wagon Company of Ince, Wigan. Along with two subsidiary firms, this company cut a large number of engines after it began purchasing from BR in 1960.

The first victims came from the Heapley Dump, followed shortly after by engines from Badnall's Wharf. All of these were of LMS origin, but before long the firm were also taking large numbers of ex-GWR types, including a pair of Hall Class 4-6-0s (4950 and 4976). Before long a variety of ex-LNER engines, including B1s and K3s were acquired. There was also a staple flow of WD 2-8-0s, Hughes 2-6-0 'Crabs' and BR Standards.

Above: *This D11/1 class 62661 was named* Gerard Powys Dewhurst, *after a Director of the Great Central Railway from 1914 until 1922. The engine came back to Gorton for scrapping in December 1960 although it had originally been withdrawn to Doncaster.* Trans Pennine Archive (E367)

Central Wagon accounted for quite a few named engines, notably Jubilee Class 4-6-0s, but supplemented by Patriot Class 45522 *Prestatyn*, Royal Scot 46129 *The Scottish Horse*, and Coronation Class 46243 *City of Lancaster*. The firm also had a yard at Barrow-in-Furness, but its operations seem even more elusive than those of the three yards in Wigan. If anyone can help with information, especially photographs, it would be most appreciated.

Top Left: *Another of the 4-4-0 classes, the D11/2s (or what came to be known as the 'Scottish Directors') was a casualty of the mass withdrawals of the late-1950s and early 1960s. Here we see 62686* The Fiery Cross, *in a line up of condemned locomotives at Cowlairs in July 1962. In the tradition of many Scottish engines their names were only painted onto the splashers. On a historical note, the Fiery Cross was used by Highlander Roderick Dhu as a mobilisation signal to call the Clans.*
Trans Pennine Archive (E385)

Bottom Left: *One of the BR works that swiftly despatched the engines sent there, was that at Stratford. Here we see a Gresley K2 Class Mogul 61754, which will follow so many other ex-LNER locomotives into the cutting shop at the end of the 1950s and the early 1960s.*
Frank Hornby (E344)

Top Right: *Introduced from 1943, the LNER N7/5 Class 0-6-2T was a post-Grouping development of the original GER-designed N7/1. They were rebuilt with a round-topped firebox at a time when plans were already being made to electrify the route from Liverpool Street where many were employed. By 3rd October 1959, things were not looking good for many of the steam engines arriving at Stratford Works. The legend chalked at the front of the locomotive (and then crossed out) indicates the build date and the lot number along with its last overhaul in 1958. As the fitters struggle with the smokebox door, it seems that 69642 has little time left to live.*
Frank Hornby (E640)

The Cohen group was another of the 'combines' who disposed of steam at a variety of locations, including Cargo Fleet on Teesside, Kettering in Northamptonshire, Morriston near Swansea and Rotherwas, Herefordshire. They also may have had other yards, including some in the Sheffield area, plus interests in other companies as well.

Steam disposal work began in 1962 and it covered engines from all six regions and many different classes. The firm also travelled to locations where engines were stored but unfit to move, and a classic example of this is 35004 *Cunard White Star Line*, which was dismantled at Eastleigh. It is impossible to present just how much work this firm did in the disposal of steam, but it should be mentioned that it also did work on diesels and multiple units as well.

The geographic spread of groups like Cohens or Thomas W. Ward meant that many of their yards did not consume more than 100 engines, but as a collective group their totals were impressive. One of these groups was Cox & Danks, who had operations in Barry, Cardiff, Brindle Heath in Manchester, two yards in North London, Sheffield and Warley and probably elsewhere as well.

Their Wadsley Bridge yard on the outskirts of Sheffield was my 'local' scrapyard, and here I witnessed a steady flow of ex-LNER types. Most of these were fairly 'run of the mill' engines, but A1 Pacifics 60119 *Patrick Stirling* and 60125 *Scottish Union* were deeply significant sightings. A trio of WD 8Fs, 90345, 90645 and 90678 were the last steam engines I witnessed there.

One yard that could be difficult to access was Alfred Draper Ltd of Hull, which seemed to be the graveyard of many freight engines, notably BR 9F 2-10-0s (38), WD 2-8-0s (205) and LMS 8F 2-8-0s (156). Draper's also made significant inroads into mixed traffic types, swallowing 111 Black Five 4-6-0s and 37 LNER B1 4-6-0s. Quite a few named engines went as well, and three that I personally witnessed were Jubilee 45568 *Western Australia*, A3 60071 *Tranquil* and A1 60157 *Great Eastern*. A separate history has been written on the Draper story, and though now out of print it is an interesting acquisition to your library, as it discusses in detail the work undertaken at Dairycoates, Neptune Street and Sculcoates.

The firm of R. S. Hayes, Bridgend, Glamorgan has already been mentioned in connection with the Birds Group who acquired the business in 1965. However, prior to that event, the yard had been cutting locomotives since August 1959. As stated, the majority of these were GWR types, of which Hayes chopped 233 into little pieces. At first the carnage was confined to tank engines, but as the years passed, the victims grew in size to include the following classes 28xx, Manor, Hall, Castle and West Country/Battle of Britain.

Hughes Bolckow are well known for their yard at Battleship Wharf on the River Blyth, but it appears that they may also have operated a small yard on the River Tees as well. The firm had cut its first locomotives on Teesside in late 1959, and it seems as though several others were cut up at locations on the BR system as they were unfit to travel. Yet it was with the end of scrapping at the Darlington Works that the biggest influx began.

The basic supply were workhorses from the North Eastern Region, including B1s (27), Q6s (27) and an unrecorded, but substantial number of J27s. Earlier books on the subject suggested that a total of 151 locomotives were handled, but it seems likely that for the company as a whole it was in excess of 200. Quite a number of named engines, ranging from Jubilee Class 45584 *North West Frontier* to A1 and A3 Pacifics were cut up, but it was for the demise of four A4s, 60001 *Sir Ronald Matthews*, 60024 *Kingfisher*, 60026 *Miles Beevor* and 60034 *Lord Faringdon*, that this yard will perhaps best be remembered.

You could expect a firm based in Norwich, like King & Son, to have been intimately connected with the despatch of East Anglian steam locomotives, but it is strange to find it cut up no less than 48 GWR types. They entered steam-breaking quite late, May 1963, by which time the Great Eastern section had largely become dieselised, so their first purchases came from the Western and London Midland regions; some coming from as far away as Didcot.

Southern Region acquisitions started in 1964, again with engines travelling for some distance, as for example M7 Class 30111 from Eastleigh. Eastern Region traction came when New England shed disposed of Class A3s 60062 *Minoru* and 60106 *Flying Fox*, along with A1 class 60129 *Guy Mannering*. Distant purchases continued down to the end, with a clutch of BR Standards and 41319 coming from storage at far away Salisbury.

One of the long running names in steam and diesel locomotive demolition was the firm of J. McWilliams, Shettlestone, Glasgow. Yet they did not begin acquiring engines until the Autumn of 1963, and at first confined their purchases to LMS types, including no less than 30 Hughes 2-6-0s. Then came the majority of the Glasgow-based Royal Scots, seven in total, and a number of Black Fives. Most significant was the firm's love of Britannia Class locomotives, and from our chosen example class, McWilliams dispatched a grand total of 22, along with a pair of Clan Class Pacifics for good measure.

However, the biggest of the Scottish yards was the Motherwell Machinery & Scrap Co. Ltd. of Wishaw, which was undoubtedly one of the 'Big Ten' private yards. They scrapped approaching 200 ex-LMS engines alone along with at least 91 BR Standards, having begun locomotive disposal with a Manning Wardle tank from the North Sunderland Railway in 1949. They then took a batch of the LT&SR tank engines (mentioned in Vol.7) from the dump at Winsford at the start of 1960, and scrapping began in earnest.

These were followed by the surviving D30 class 4-4-0s that were still working in Scotland at the end of 1959. Numerous Scottish types followed, but four A4s, six A2s, Clan 72009 and five Britannia Class engines were amongst the named locomotives that died at Wishaw.

The Slag Reduction Group had a number of yards where locomotive scrapping took place although many of these were simply concerned with cutting up industrial engines. It had several sites concerned with the disposal of BR engines, the main ones being at Barrow-in-Furness, Briton Ferry, Rotherham and Swansea. At Rotherham, the group was also firmly connected with Peter Woods Ltd. and Balborough Metals Ltd. and some engines acquired for other Slag Reduction sites were sent there instead.

The company handled a steady progression of engines, surprisingly including a number of Southern types of which Merchant Navy Pacifics 35002 *Union Castle* and 35015 *Rotterdam Lloyd* are worthy of note.

Above: *An N2 keeps company with fellow ex-GNR locomotive J50/2 Class 0-6-0 68929 on death row at Doncaster. The 'Plant' stopped cutting steam engines in 1964, but started once again on diesels and electrics through the 1970s and 1980s.*
Trans Pennine Archive (E396)

More firmly in SR territory another yard associated with Slag Reduction/Peter Woods, was the firm of Settle-Speakman Ltd. of Queensborough on the former South Eastern & Chatham line to Sheerness. It took mainly Southern and Standard classes, but its notable victims included four Battle of Britain/West Country light Pacifics and a number of Q Class 0-6-0s.

The biggest of all the groups was the firm of Thomas W. Ward whose headquarters were in Sheffield. This firm was intimately associated with breaking heavy plant, and their activities stretched from the demolition of the former Cammell Laird Steel Tyre Rolling Mill at Penistone to dismantling the Rosedale Iron Railway in North Yorkshire. Sheffield's trams were amongst its many victims, as were hundreds of obsolete steam locomotives that the National Coal Board decided to scrap after the industry was nationalised.

The list on page 45 shows the main locations where T.W. Ward Ltd. are known to have had yards handling BR steam engines, but it would not surprise me to discover that they had other locations as well. Work began in earnest in 1959, as engines from dumps in Derbyshire and Manchester arrived. But it also appeared that part-cut locomotives had been arriving from Derby, Gorton and Wolverhampton from as early as 1957. By far the biggest operations were those found at Beighton and Killamarsh, although Attercliffe and Broughton Lane were all busy.

Each of these were in the heartland of British steel-making, South Yorkshire, but the firm had other locations including yards at Inverkeithing and Wishaw in Scotland and at Briton Ferry, Cardiff and Newport in Wales as well as various places in England.

As mentioned earlier, the records of this firm's activities are still supposed to exist, and we remain hopeful that one day these will be made available. For the present we can mention that the Beighton and Killamarsh yards between them took over 300 LMS types and approaching 100 BR Standards or WD types. Included in this total were no less than 12 Britannia Class Pacifics, five at Beighton, five at Inverkeithing and two engines at Killamarsh. Beighton and Killamarsh consumed 50 9F 2-10-0s, but they missed out on a tendered bid for five Clan Class 4-6-0s in the Autumn of 1963, and these were amongst the last engines to be cut up at Darlington Works in 1964.

The firm's yard at Grays in Essex had fun with a number of Southern designs, including classes Q and U. Briton Ferry chomped its way through a variety of GWR types, but it also handled a dozen M7 tank engines from the Southern Region as well.

Yet, without any doubt, the greatest yard of all was noted more for the number of engines it did not cut as opposed to those it did. I refer of course to the firm of Woodham Brothers of Barry Island, Wales. It cannot be emphasised how important this yard became, but it is a story well told in a variety of books and magazine articles that have appeared over the years, and one that has also been told in Volume 7 of this series and *Steam For Scrap - The Complete Story*. Also worthy of study, is the book *The Barry Scrapyard: The Preservation Miracle* by Alan Warren and published by David & Charles.

The wide number of photographs that are found in this book will also tell the story far better than any words I could write, and I think it is safe to say that over the years Agfa, Kodak and a host of other film manufacturers will have made a tidy profit on sales of their products that enthusiasts acquired to record the passing scene.

I first saw the Barry dump early in 1968, although I did not then appreciate the role it was to play in the re-birth of British steam. By the time I made my next visit to the yard in 1971, steam had been dead for almost three years on BR, and already preservation candidates were being prepared for their departure to railway preservation centres around the country.

The first to leave had been ex-LMS 4F 0-6-0 43924, which had ironically travelled to my home county of the West Riding of Yorkshire, where it would settle on the Keighley & Worth Valley Railway. My last visit to the yard saw my taking photographs of an engine that I had seen many times during my youth, BR Standard Class 2MT 2-6-0 78022. I photographed it as a wreck over the Easter weekend in 1975, but 17-years on was privileged to witness the fully refurbished engine roll out of the Keighley & Worth Valley workshops in Haworth on Friday 16th October 1992.

Many other readers will be able to associate similar stories with locomotives that have come out of Barry, the majority of which have now been re-built and put back into service on preserved railways up and down the land. Today, a new generation of steam enthusiast is turning its hand to building brand new locomotives, notably from classes that did not survive the cull of BR steam, but the basis for all their labours is undoubtedly found in Barry.

The story needs widening considerably, and there is no doubt that future volumes in this series can be justified. Of course, the main difficulty is that of suitable colour illustrations, but it should be borne in mind that when we did the original books, we had quite a task to find enough colour images to provide us with illustrations for the cover. Now we have dedicated two complete books to the story, and done so in full colour.

Undoubtedly, there is more illustrative material still out there to be found, and I would appeal to readers to help us trace these images and add them to the catalogue. The opportunity to share these with fellow enthusiasts is a big reward, but so too is the chance to fill in those gaps in the record!

Above: *The ex-North Eastern Railway works at Darlington was in full swing during the 1950s building both steam and the replacement diesel classes. In total 75 BR Standards started their days in the Darlington erection shops. Some were also to be sent there for scrapping too, among them was Clan Pacific 72002* Clan Campbell. *Seen on 19th September 1963 she was just over ten years old but was still heading for oblivion. As an early withdrawal candidate she is of course rarely seen in colour, and whilst this view is not on the sunniest of days it is included for rarity value. Some of the BR Standards are not thought to have been recorded in colour; for example, one notable collector has been searching for over 25 years for a shot of 9F 92193. (Please make contact with us if you can help?)*
Strathwood Library Collection (B342)

It is a sadly depressing subject, especially when one considers the wastage of a valuable resource. Given our discussion of the figures, the reader will be able to pose his or her own questions, and amongst these must be the important issue of the 999 BR Standards. Surely, these were built a generation too late, and therefore a resource that was sadly wasted?

Take for example the biggest of all BR Standards (both in size and number) the 9F 2-10-0s. Of these no less than 122 had a working life of under ten years, 32 of these did under seven years and eight less than five years. Even the eldest members of the class were to be used for a period of not much more than 14 years, less than a third of their projected lifespan. Survivors of the class have now worked longer in preservation than they did in real life!

Although I am as passionate about steam as anyone, my study of the subject has made me realise that the Standard locomotive programme came far too late, and dieselisation with its many pilot classes was hastily rushed in. Given the advantages of electric traction today, one wonders what would have been the case if the programme had been implemented much earlier. The Southern Railway and LNER had shown the way with their various, albeit incompatible, schemes in the 1930s and these deserved greater consideration by BR after it was formed.

However, steam was perpetuated for a further decade, before the bean crunchers decided it was time for a change. The consequence therefore was not an orderly and logical withdrawal and replacement programme, but an inexcusable and unjustified mass slaughter!

Left: *By 1966 the folly of it all was plain to see as we find here at Ayr (67C) with Standard Class 5MT 4-6-0 keeping company in the scrap line with not only a Stanier Black Five, but even the diesel rail-bus (just seen on the left) is also already past its 'sell by date'. Even though 73145 was built as recently as January 1957, with so called modern 'British Caprotti' valve gear, the end has come just nine years later. What a waste indeed!*
Douglas Paul (B237)

Top Right: *Built in 1957 as a product of Crewe Works, BR Standard 9F 2-10-0 92134 enjoyed only a short working life. It was badly neglected in her latter years with BR as can be seen here in 1968, a year after her arrival at Barry. It is ironic that many of the images we have at certain places were not always taken in the best of locations or conditions, but yet they are so valuable that they have to be included for their rarity; as for example this side of the Barry yard. Later the 9F would be moved to other parts of the yard where it was more commonly photographed.*
Len Smith (B310)

Bottom Right: *As if to prove the point, here we see Swindon-built 9F 92214 among a few of the many survivors that found their way to Barry. Clearly the practicalities of moving the locomotives into a position where they could be cut up was always going to be a task in itself. Happily it was so much easier to shunt wagons and to cut them up instead. But when this shot was taken from a location so familiar to us all, who could have known how it would all end?* Win Wall, Strathwood Library Collection (B311)

Above: *The last BR-built steam engine to be scrapped as a result of the withdrawal of steam in 1968 was Standard 9F 92085. Seen at Barry with many of its parts robbed for use on other engines, this 2-10-0 was finally broken up in July 1980.* Nick Gledhill (B343)

EVERY PICTURE is worth a thousand words, or so they say, and thanks to the combined talents of photographers who have supplied material to both the Strathwood and Trans-Pennine archives, we have a lot to say in future volumes. Of course it would not have been possible to tell this story without the kind co-operation of the contributors named in the credits shown in this book. To those and all those who captured British Railways In Colour, we say a massive thank you! However mere words are never enough, and we hope that the ongoing series will provide a testimony to their far-sighted work.

In conclusion, can we offer a reminder that all of these published shots are available to purchase as superb duplicate slide copies direct from Strathwood. The code number at the end of each slide indicates its catalogue number, and also the name of the photographer whose work we felt warranted inclusion.

To get your copy of the extensive catalogue listing of these and many thousands of other shots available in fabulous colour, please send £5.00 to: -

Strathwood Limited
Kirkland House, Bruce Street, Whithorn.
Dumfries & Galloway DG8 8PY
Or visit the websites: -
www.strathwood.com or www.railwayslide.co.uk.

In return we will send the collector's catalogue, complete with sample slide, post free to UK addresses (overseas add £2.50).